Sand

Monica Halpern

Where Can You Find Sand?

You've probably played with sand in a sandbox. Where else can you find sand?

You can find sand all over. You can find sand on a beach. You can find sand in a desert. Sand can also be buried beneath the soil. Sand can be almost anywhere, but what is it? Where does it come from? What can you do with it?

Many people like to relax on a sandy beach.

Workers dig sand out of the ground.

Sand covers most of this desert.

What Is Sand?

Most sand is made from rocks. Over a long period of time, wind and rain and ice beat against the rocks. Pieces of rocks are broken off. These pieces are gradually ground down into smaller and smaller pieces. Finally, the pieces turn into tiny grains of sand.

The color of sand depends on the material from which it is made. White sand is made from coral. Coral reefs lie under the warm ocean waters near the Equator. Over a long period of time, waves and wind break the coral into tiny grains of very white sand.

coral

Black sand is made from lava. When a volcano erupts, hot lava pours down its sides. The hot lava turns into hard, shiny, black rock when it cools. Over a long period of time, the black rock is ground down into grains of black sand.

lava

Golden sand is made from a kind of quartz. Quartz is a mineral that can be found in rocks. When rocks with this kind of quartz in them are ground down, tiny pieces of golden sand are made. Other minerals make different colored sand.

quartz

Sand can be made up of several different materials. Sand might be a mix of coral and rock or rock and lava. Sand made from different materials will be a mix of colors.

Sand comes in different shapes and sizes, too. Grains of sand can be round or pointy. The photograph below shows a close-up view of grains of sand.

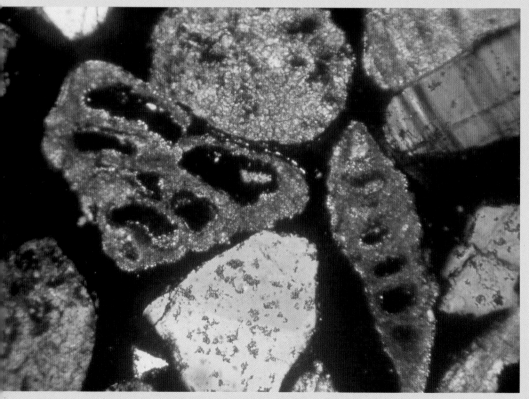

Grains of sand come in many different colors and shapes.

Sand is different from dirt. Grains of dirt are smaller than grains of sand. If you pour water into a bowl of dirt, the water will soak into the dirt very slowly. If you pour water into a bowl of sand, it will run right through the sand. This happens because there are larger spaces between the grains of sand than between the grains of dirt.

sand   dirt

Water soaks faster through sand than through dirt.

9

How Does Sand Move Around?

Sand can be moved from one place to another in three different ways. It can be moved by water, wind, and ice.

The water in rivers and streams moves sand. As a river flows over the land it picks up sand. When the water slows down, the sand sinks.

Ocean waves move sand. They can move sand from one beach to another. Waves can move sand from the ocean floor to the shore and back to the ocean floor again. During a storm, big waves can move large amounts of sand.

Strong winds move sand across beaches and desert lands, too. The winds form giant piles of sand called sand dunes. Winds can also form ripples on the sand's surface.

Ice can move sand, too. Sometimes, sand is trapped in the ice. When the ice melts, the sand stays on land or drops into the sea. Then wind and waves begin their work again.

What Can You Do With Sand?

People use sand in many different ways. Some people have fun with sand on the beach.

Some people use sand at work. Workers blow sand on old buildings to get the dirt off. Artists use sand to make glass.

Sand is also used to keep people safe. Workers sprinkle sand over icy roads to make them less slippery. People pile bags of sand along the edge of a river. The sand keeps the river from flooding.

These bags of sand will stop the river from flooding.

A worker cleans a building by blowing sand on it.

An artist uses sand to make glass art.

Kids build sand castles at the beach.

The next time you are on a beach, look closely at the sand. Remember that every grain of sand has a story. See if you can figure out what the sand was made from or how it may have gotten there.